Before you start ...

1 Gather together everything you need for the activity using the equipment list at the top of each page. You can use water-based paint for nearly all the activities – a thick mixture works best.

2 Cover your worktable with newspaper and wear an apron to protect your clothes.

3 Read all the instructions carefully. Practice printing on scrap paper first.

4 Be very careful with scissors and knives. Only use them if an adult is there to help you.

5 When you have finished an activity, wash your hands and put everything away.

A DK PUBLISHING BOOK

Written and edited by Lara Tankel and Dawn Sirett
Art Editors Mandy Earey and Mary Sandberg
Additional design Veneta Altham
Deputy Managing Art Editor C. David Gillingwater
US Editor Camela Decaire
Production Fiona Baxter
Dib, Dab, and Dob made by Wilfrid Wood
Photography by Alex Wilson and Norman Hollands
Illustrations by Peter Kavanagh

First American Edition, 1997
2 4 6 8 10 9 7 5 3 1

Published in the United States by DK Publishing, Inc.
95 Madison Avenue, New York, New York 10016

Copyright © 1997 Dorling Kindersley Limited, London
Visit us on the World Wide Web at http://www.dk.com

Published in Great Britain by Dorling Kindersley Ltd.

A CIP catalog record for this book is available from the Library of Congress.

ISBN 0-7894-1521-6

Color reproduction by Colourscan, Singapore
Printed and bound in Hong Kong by Imago

PLAY AND LEARN
Printing Things

With Dib, Dab, and Dob

leaves paint paintbrush construction paper

Print leaf patterns

Paint the
back of a leaf.

Press it onto
some paper.

Peel the
leaf back.

Try decorating notebooks or gift boxes with leaf prints.

vegetables knife saucer paint  construction paper

Print vegetable shapes

Ask an adult to cut some vegetables in half.

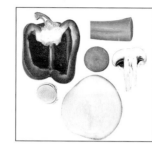

Pour some paint in a saucer.

Vegetable variety

Try printing on a birthday card, a picture frame, or a box. You can make all sorts of fun patterns.

We printed one vegetable over another to make this face.

 modeling clay plastic knife sponge  saucer paint

Print with modeling clay

Shape some
clay and make
marks in it with
a plastic knife.

Put a sponge on a
saucer and pour paint
on the sponge.

Press the
clay into the
sponge and
then onto
tissue paper

construction paper   paint   paintbrush

Find a hidden butterfly

Fold a sheet of paper in half. Open it up and dab thick paint on one side.

Fold it in half again and gently press it down.

 paint saucer flowerpots

Hand- and footprints on pots

Pour some paint in a saucer. Press your hand or foot into the paint.

Wear old clothes when you print like this.

Then press your hand or foot onto a flowerpot. Ask a friend to hold the pot steady.

Print all around the pot using different colors. You can do fingerprints, too.

construction paper

scissors

thick cardboard

plain T-shirt

Stencil a T-shirt

Ask an adult to fold a sheet of paper in quarters and to cut shapes out of it.

Slide a sheet of thick cardboard into a T-shirt.* Then tape your paper with cutouts to the front.

*The thick cardboard stops the paint from soaking through.

masking tape

sponge

fabric paint

Dip a sponge into some fabric paint. Then dab the paint into the cutout, or stencil, holes.

When the paint is dry, lift off the stencil.

Ready to wear

Remember to check the washing instructions on your fabric paint.